Now I Know

Baby Animals

Written by Susan Kuchalla
Illustrated by Joel Snyder

Troll Associates

Library of Congress Cataloging in Publication Data

Kuchalla, Susan.
  Baby animals.

  (Now I know)
  Summary: Brief text and pictures introduce several
baby animals and show how they play and learn.
  1. Animals, Infancy of—Juvenile literature.
[1. Animals—Infancy] I. Snyder, Joel, ill.
II. Title.
QL763.K82   599.03 '9   81-11434
ISBN 0-89375-666-0   AACR2
ISBN 0-89375-667-9 (pbk.)

Baby animals are very special!

A kid is a baby goat.

A kitten is a baby cat.

And a colt is a baby horse.

Baby animals are many different sizes.

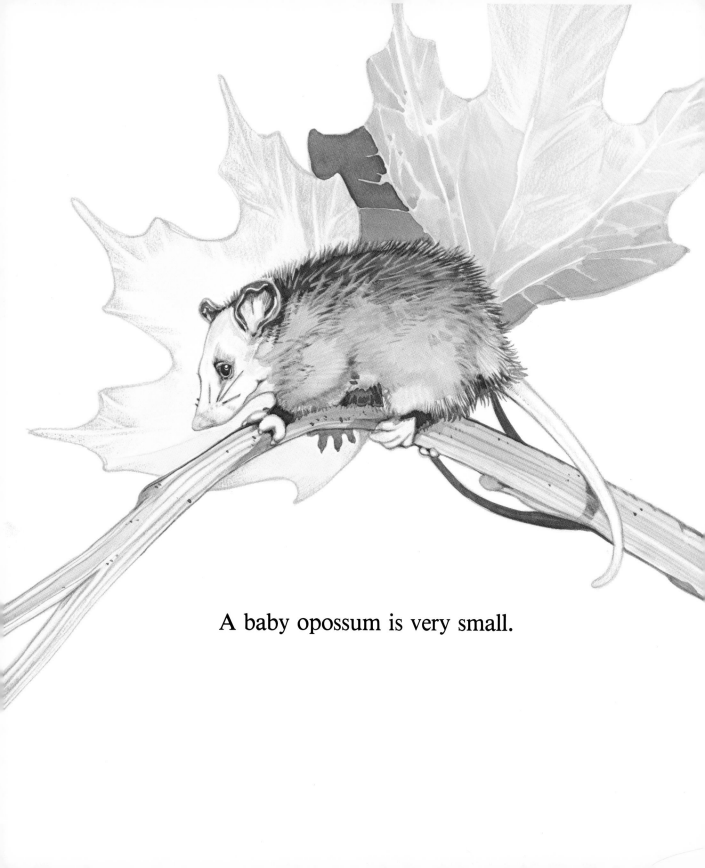

A baby opossum is very small.

But a baby elephant is very big.

It likes to follow its mother around.

And it likes to be hugged!

Some baby animals grow fast.
It takes a puppy one year to grow up.

But it takes some baby animals
twenty years to grow up!

All baby animals like to play.

Baby elephants have water fights. *Whoosh!*

Baby lambs play follow-the-leader.

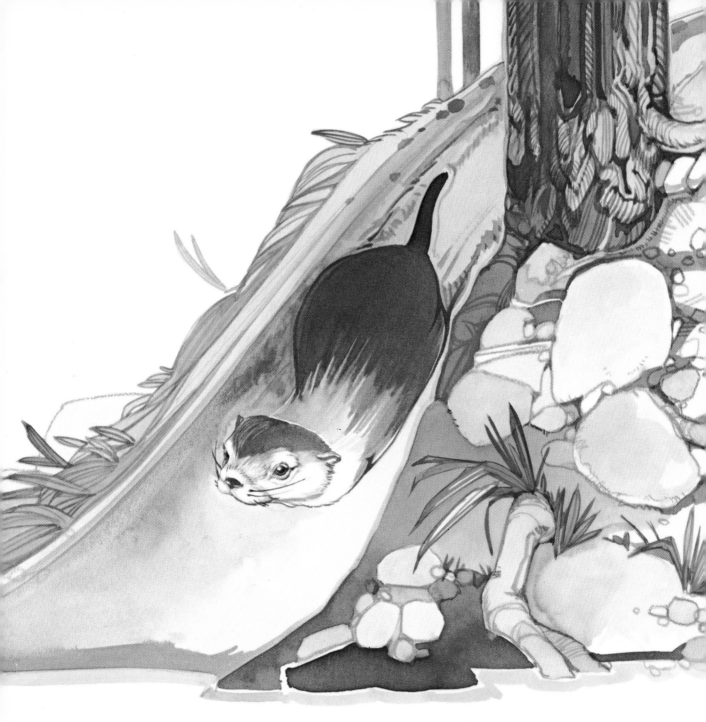

And baby otters like to slide down hills.

But baby animals must learn, too.

Some learn how to swim.

All baby animals must learn how to find food.

These cubs are baby tigers.
They are learning when to stay quiet.

And they are learning where to look for food.

Every grown-up animal was once a baby.

A furry opossum was once tiny and helpless.

Dogs and cats were once puppies and kittens.

And even a mighty tiger . . .

. . . was once a playful baby.

Baby animals are very special!